Naming Money

By Nick Rebman

level 1
little blue readers

www.littlebluehousebooks.com

Little Blue House is distributed by North Star Editions:
sales@northstareditions.com | 888-417-0195

Produced for Little Blue House by Red Line Editorial.

Photographs ©: Shutterstock Images, cover, 4, 7, 8–9, 11, 12–13, 15, 16 (top left), 16 (top right), 16 (bottom left), 16 (bottom right)

Library of Congress Control Number: 2020900810

ISBN
978-1-64619-167-3 (hardcover)
978-1-64619-201-4 (paperback)
978-1-64619-269-4 (ebook pdf)
978-1-64619-235-9 (hosted ebook)

Printed in the United States of America
Mankato, MN
012021

About the Author

Nick Rebman enjoys reading, walking his dog, and collecting coins from around the world. He lives in Minnesota.

Table of Contents

Naming Money

I see pennies.

I see nickels.

I see dimes.

I see quarters.

quarter

I see dollars.

I see money.

money

Glossary

dimes

pennies

nickels

quarters

Index